Early CSX Diesels

SD35 - SDP35 - SD40-2 - SD45-2 - GP30 - MP15AC

AN ILLUSTRATED STUDY

FOR GRANDMA RUTH

Table of Contents

CSX MP15AC #1134

MP15AC ROSTER

SCL/L:N
GEORGIA • CLINCHFIELD
WEST POINT ROUTE

SEABOARD
SYSTEM

CSX
TRANSPORTATION

SEABOARD COAST LINE

Road Number	Builder Date	Builder Number
4000-4019	10/77	777024-1 to 20
4200-4224	2/78	777032-1 to 25

FAMILY LINES SYSTEM

Road Number	Builder Date	Builder Number
4200-4224	10/77	777024-1 to 20
4200-4224	2/78	777032-1 to 25

L&N

Road Number	Builder Date	Builder Number
4225-4234	3/78	777038-1 to 10

SEABOARD SYSTEM

Road Number	Builder Date	Builder Number
4200-4224	10/77	777024-1 to 20
4200-4224	2/78	777032-1 to 25
4225-4234	3/78	777038-1 to 10

MP15AC

After the SW1500 program was completed, EMD build the MP15 series of locomotives as a locomotive to not only work in Yards, but be a road switcher as well. Riding on Blomberg trucks, it had a larger fuel tank compared to the earlier SW1500. Unfortunately these locomotives did not come with toilets, and some States required toilets to be used as leading units or in lashups. Even though a higher price tag was also a factor, they had decent sales numbers. In the SCL/SBD era, they could be found in lashups on through freights as well as locals and seen in Yards.

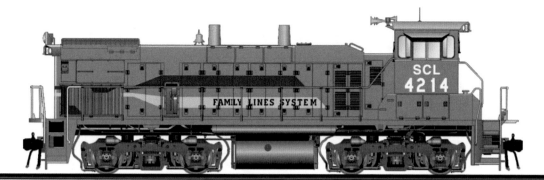

SEABOARD COAST LINE MP15AC #4214,

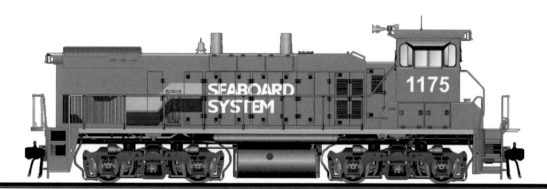

SEABOARD SYSTEM MP15AC #1175
Renumbered after creation of CSX

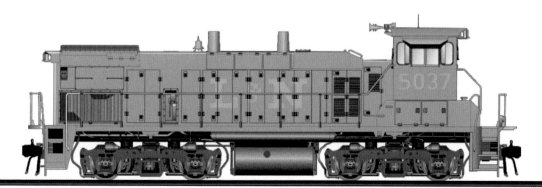

LOUISVILLE & NASHVILLE MP15AC #5037

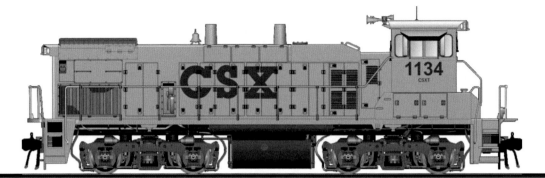

CSX MP15AC #1134

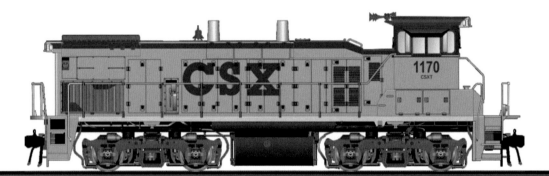

CSX MP15AC #1170

CSX MP15AC #1192

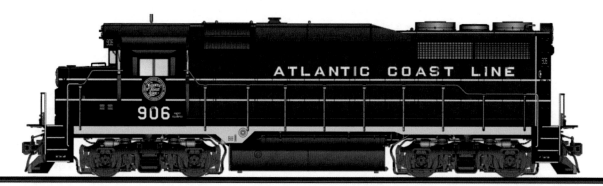

ATLANTIC COAST LINE GP30 #906

GP-30 ROSTER

SEABOARD AIR LINE

Road Number	Builder Date	Builder Number
500-533	11/62-1/63	EMD 27928-61
534		EMD 27462

ATLANTIC COAST LINE

Road Number	Builder Date	Builder Number
900-908	1/63	EMD 27989-27997

CHESAPEAKE & OHIO

Road Number	Builder Date	Builder Number
3000-3015	8/62-12/62	EMD 27798-99, 27584-97
3016-3047	8-10/63	EMD 28410-11, 28494-523

BALTIMORE & OHIO

Road Number	Builder Date	Builder Number
6900-6972	10-12/62	EMD 27617-27689
6973-6976	1/63	EMD 27690-27693

LOUISVILLE & NASHVILLE

Road Number	Builder Date	Builder Number
1000-1028	6-12/62	27399-27427
1029-1048	5-9/63	27752-27771
1049-1057	10-11/63	28645-28653

(Other locomotives were purchased or leased from other railroads for L&N)
*#1014 was EMD's 25,000th locomotive *#1057 was the last GP30 ever built.

GP30

Designed to compete with General Electric's brand new U-25B, the GP30 had a very unique design along its cab roof. This extra space allowed for the Turbo charger, central air system and the electrical cabinet right behind the cab. The ACL's order did not have dynamic brakes, but kept the same style as the other units built. Many railroads purchased the units, both larger roads and smaller. The GP30 was only built until late 1963. The Chessie System rebuilt their locomotives into what became GP30m's.

GP30's

of the Seaboard and Atlantic Coast Line

Seaboard Air Line

Big changes came to the north end of the railroad in 1962, as the older lashups of GP9's and their sisters from a decade before were beginning to be replaced. They were quickly falling out of favor with the arrival of the GP30's from EMD. Having 2,250 horsepower, they were more powerful and had a very distinct look about them. First used on Hamlet, NC. to Richmond, VA. freights in November of that year, they allowed the older FT units to be traded in to EMD for the second batch of GP30's. South of Savannah, GA, it took a while for the new locomotives to show up as Jacksonville Shops were the home of most of the ALCO fleet.

They worked on all 5 lines which left Hamlet and could be seen along with older locomotives in consist arriving and terminating there. At the time of the merger in 1967, they were renumbered into a new series and repainted into the black and yellow scheme of the new Seaboard Coast Line Railroad during the next few years.

Atlantic Coast Line

When ACL purchased their new GP30's, they chose the option of not having Dynamic Brakes installed. This was due to the flat as a pancake profile (for the most part) of the railroad's race track along the Southeastern Coast between Richmond, VA. and Tampa, FL. They also had ATC shoes installed as all ACL locomotives in mainline service did. The extra light packages found on Coast Line locomotives were installed.

The GP30's were early on assigned to Trains 109-110 between Richmond, VA. and Jacksonville, FL. When the GP35's arrived in 1963, they were often joined with the GP30's and other units as the heavy tonnage which made up trains proved too much even on relatively flat track profiles. In 1976, the ex- ACL GP30's were transferred to the L&N as they were power short at the time.

Some of the SCL units made it into Family Lines, Seaboard System and even a few CSX schemes.

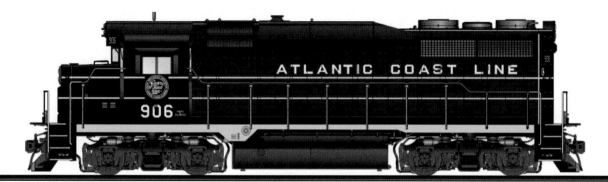

ATLANTIC COAST LINE GP30 #906

SEABOARD COAST LINE GP30 #1343

CLINCHFIELD GP30 #1350
In Family Lines Paint

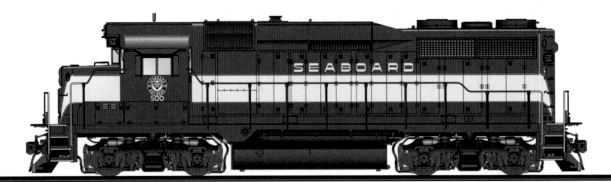

SEABOARD AIR LINE GP30 #500

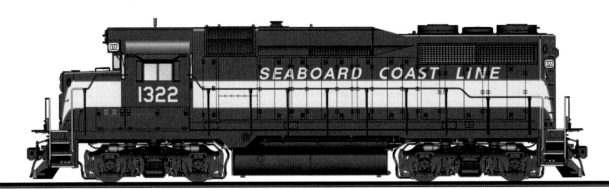

SEABOARD COAST LINE GP30 #1322
In the Split Image scheme.

SEABOARD COAST LINE GP30 #1339

CSX GP30 #4055

SEABOARD SYSTEM GP30 #1389

CLINCHFIELD GP30 #1350
In Family Lines Paint

CHESAPEAKE & OHIO GP30 #3001

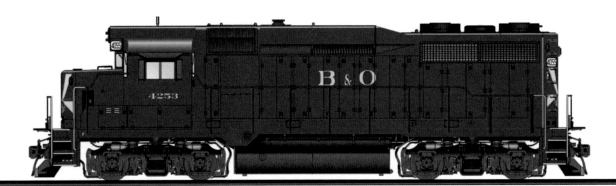

BALTIMORE & OHIO GP30 #4253

CHESAPEAKE & OHIO GP30 #4203
In Chessie System Paint.

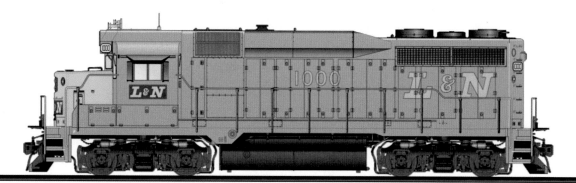

LOUISVILLE & NASHVILLE GP30 #1000

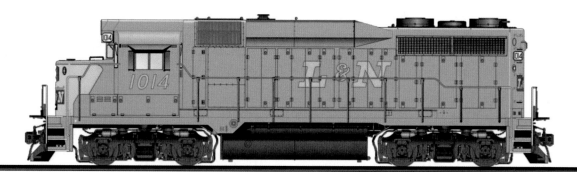

LOUISVILLE & NASHVILLE GP30 #1014

CHESAPEAKE & OHIO GP30 #3002

CSX SD35 #4586

SD35 ROSTER

ATLANTIC COAST LINE

Road Number	Builder Date	Builder Number
1000-1023	6/64-9-65	*various separate orders*

SEABOARD COAST LINE

Road Number	Builder Date	Builder Number
1900-1910	6,11,12/64	EMD 29035-38, 29594-600
1911-1923	9/65	EMD 30518-30
1950-1970	Steam Generator removed, re#. from #600-620	

LOUISVILLE & NASHVILLE* *EX-SCL UNITS

Road Number	Builder Date	Builder Number
1279-1283		EMD 29037-38, 29597 & 99
1283-1288		EMD 30518, 30526-30

BALTIMORE & OHIO

Road Number	Builder Date	Builder Number
7400-7419	7-10/64	29408-29427
7437-7440	9/65	30706-30709

CHESAPEAKE & OHIO

Road Number	Builder Date	Builder Number
7420-7431	9-11/64	29428-29439

WESTERN MARYLAND

Road Number	Builder Date	Builder Number
7432-7436	12/64	29890-29894

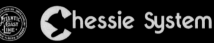

SD35

Developing 2,500 horsepower, the SD35 shared a similar frame with the SD-28. Having a fuel tank with 3,000 gals and a length of 60 feet, 8.5 inches. It was developed on the heals of the EMD SD40, and sold a total of 360 locomotives. They were built between June, 1964 and January, 1966.

Louisville & Nashville locomotives came from the Seaboard Coast Line. The group saw many paint schemes, including early CSX schemes in blue and gray.

SD35'S

of the Atlantic Coast Line

In stark contrast to the North-South mainline running nearly the length of the South Atlantic coast, the Western Division of the ACL had its fair share of grades. This area covered the rails from Waycross, GA to Birmingham, AL. and Atlanta, GA. The SD35's came to the ACL in 3 batches, between June, 1964 until August the following year. It was here especially where the mechanical forces fell in love with them, although they were used all over the system. Piggyback trains and Manifest trains could be found with these locomotives up front or in the consist powering them due to their power.

They were based out of Waycross, GA, but went in all directions from there, even all the way north to Richmond, VA. The SD35's were often used with other six-axle power. In the 1970's, 10 of these units joined their GP30 sisters over on L&N rails. By the early 80's, L&N removed them from road service and sent them to work in the Yards across the system.

They would go on to see various paint schemes, including all the way up to early CSX schemes.

BALTIMORE & OHIO SD35 #7402

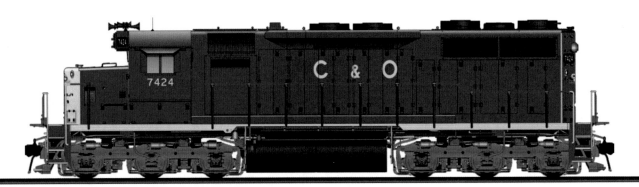

CHESAPEAKE & OHIO SD35 #7424

BALTIMORE & OHIO SD35 #7406
In Chessie System paint.

WESTERN MARYLAND SD35 #7436
In Chessie System paint.

WESTERN MARYLAND SD35 #7432

WESTERN MARYLAND SD35 #7435

ATLANTIC COAST LINE SD35 #1001

SEABOARD COAST LINE SD35 #1920

SEABOARD COAST LINE SD35 #1920

SEABOARD SYSTEM SD35 #4523
Painted in Family Lines colors

SEABOARD SYSTEM SD35 #4532

CSX SD35 #4519

SCL SDP35 #618
Painted in the SCL" Split image" scheme

SDP35 ROSTER

ATLANTIC COAST LINE

Road Number	Builder Date	Builder Number
1099	9/65	EMD 30531

SEABOARD AIR LINE

Road Number	Builder Date	Builder Number
1100-1119	7-11/64	EMD 29339-58

SEABOARD COAST LINE

Road Number	Builder Date	Builder Number
600	9/65	EMD 30531
601-620	7-11/64	EMD 29339-58

LOUISVILLE & NASHVILLE

Road Number	Builder Date	Builder Number
1700–1703	9/65	30454-30457

SDP35

In order to replace the aging locomotives from two decades past, the ACL, SAL and L&N purchased the SDP35. On the SAL, they were excellent in both passenger and hotshot and piggyback service. In later years after Amtrak took over, the SCL gutted the boiler area of the locomotive and renumbered them, they were used in yard service at many hump yards across the system. The L&N had little use for them in passenger service when received, as many of their passenger trains had been annulled. They too removed the passenger train equipment and installed remote locomotive controls in the area and were used as remote controlled locomotives until 1969. Some were rebuilt by the Seaboard System, (SD35's were also used in this program) being designated H-15's, of which 8 were built. They also served CSX late in life.

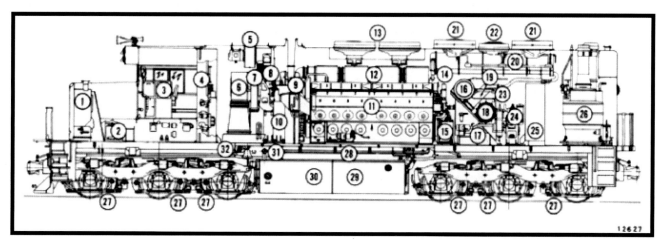

General Arrangement - SDP35

(Information shown is that of the SD35. So similar were these two locomotives EMD published the same Operator's manual)

1. Sand Box
2. Battery
3. Loco. Controls
4. No.1 Electrical Cabinet
5. Inertial Separator
6. Traction Motor Blower
7. Generator Blower
8. Auxiliary Generator
9. Turbocharger

10. Main Generator
11. Engine 16-567D3A
12. Exhaust Manifold
13. Dyn. Brake Fans
14. Engine Governor
15. Lube Oil Strainer
16. Engine Water Tank
17. Fuel Pump
18. Lube Oil Filters

19. Lube Oil Cooler
20. Radiators
21. 48" Fan and Motor
22. 36" Fan and Motor
23. Fuel Filter
24. Air Compressor
25. No. 2 Electrical Cabinet
26. Steam Generator
27. Traction Motors

28. Main Air Reservoir
29. Water Tank
30. Fuel Tank
31. Fuel Filler Opening
32. Emergency Fuel
    Cutoff Button

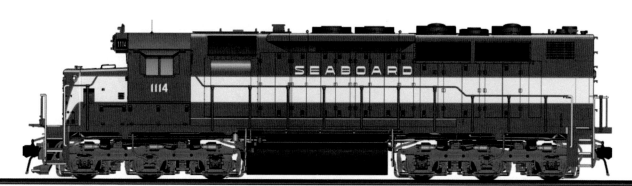

SEABOARD AIR LINE SDP35 #1114
On Display in Hamlet, NC

ATLANTIC COAST LINE SDP35 #1099

SEABOARD COAST LINE SDP35 #1953

SEABOARD SYSTEM SDP35 #4542

LOUISVILLE & NASHVILLE SDP35# 1222

LOUISVILLE & NASHVILLE SDP35# 1289
Painted in Family Lines System paint.

CSX SDP35 #4524

SDP35'S
of the Seaboard and Atlantic Coast Line

By the early 1960's, Seaboard's and ACL passenger diesels were beginning to show their age. Some of the locomotives had been in service since the late 1930's, and most had been in service two decades.

The railroads at this time had seen the writing on the wall for passenger service, each year losing more and more money on them. The Seaboard knew the end of the passenger train era was just around the corner, but wisely from a financial standpoint didn't want to purchase replacement locomotives used just in that service.

It was decided by SAL's management to purchase 20 of EMD's latest passenger diesel. This unique locomotive was basically a SD35, but with a higher gear ratio and a steam boiler to handle passenger train assignments. This would benefit current operations by allowing the railroad to retire some of their most worn equipment, and due to the higher speed of 89 mph., could be used in fast freight service when not in front of passenger trains.

Seaboard's SDP35's locomotives were delivered to Hamlet, NC where on August 1st, 1964 one of them pulled Train #4 Northbound out of town.

#1100-1105 were later assigned to Trains 9 and 10, "The Palmland" between Richmond, VA. and Miami, Fl.

The others were normally assigned to freight service, but did run sometimes on the section of the "Silver Comet" between Hamlet, NC and Birmingham, Ala.

At the time of the merger between the SAL and the ACL, ACL's lone SDP35 was renumbered to match those of her sisters in pullman green and yellow paint in a new numbering series of #601-#620. They would be renumbered a few times afterwards. In the mid-1970's, some were assigned to the L&N. By the Seaboard System era, they were assigned to Hump and Yard Service.

#1114 has been cosmetically restored and is on display at the Train Station in Hamlet, NC where her and her sisters were delivered to their new owners back in 1964.

ROUTE OF THE

Silver Comet

CSX SD40-2 #8246

SD40-2 ROSTER

SEABOARD COAST LINE

Road Number	Builder Date	Builder Number
8040-8066	6/80	786208-1 to 27
8087-8094	6/80	796334-1 to 8
8130	6/80	80709-1

LOUISVILLE & NASHVILLE

Road Number	Builder Date	Builder Number
8000-8033	3-4/79	786167-01 to 34
8034-8039	8/79	786209-01 to 06
8067-8086	10-11/79	786287-01 to 20
8095-8115	5-6/80	796329-01 to 21
8116-8126	8/80	786268-01 to 11
8133-8062	9/81	816010-01 to 30
3554-3683	10-12/74	74644-1 to 30
3584-3605	9/77	776023-01 to 22
3606-3609	10-12/74	776026-01 to 4
3610-3613	10-12/74	776027-01 to 4

CC&O (CLINCHFIELD)

Road Number	Builder Date	Builder Number
8127 - 8129	8/88	796335-1 to 3
8131 & 8132	9/81	816009-1, 817012-1

B&O (CHESSIE SYSTEM)

Road Number	Builder Date	Builder Number
7600-7609	1-2/77	767033-1 to 10
7610-7619	2/77	767033-11 to 20

ONEIDA & WESTERN SD40-2 #9957

SD40-2's

of the Oneida & Western

The Oneida & Western Railroad never owned an actual railroad itself, but was the result of a Company needing transportation but could not find it. So, in the 1970's, the Shamrock Coal Company purchased their own locomotive fleet of 8 SD40-2's from EMD. They were built to the same standards as the L&N's recent order.

The L&N was unable to guarantee delivery of the coal company's trains to their customer's powerplants due to a shortage of motive power. The energy crisis of the 1970's led to more coal fired power plants being built across the country, but especially in the South. This drove the price of coal up, and high demand for locomotives to move it.

The L&N agreed to lower rates for Shamrock if they provided their own power, and the lime green and dark green units were born.

The railroad was named after the Oneida & Western Railroad, a defunct shortline in East Tennessee from many years before. The locomotives, along with two cabooses and two sets of 72 car rotary dump hopper cars made up the rolling stock. L&N crews operated the trains on their lines. By the 1980's, things changed on the regulatory spectrum of the railroad business. Prices came back down, and CSX took control of the shipments. By 1987, the two tone green locomotives were not needed, and were sold off. The locomotives were all sold to the British Columbia Railway in Canada.

O&W Roster Information

Road Number	Builder Date	Builder /Frame Number
9950-9957	9/79	786246-1/8

SEABOARD COAST LINE SD40-2 #8065
Painted in Family Lines System paint.

SEABOARD SYSTEM SD40-2 #3585

BALTIMORE & OHIO SD40-2 #7600
Painted in Chessie System paint.

CLINCHFIELD SD45-2 #3610

SD45-2 ROSTER

SEABOARD COAST LINE

Road Number	Builder Date	Builder Number
2045-2059	8-9/74	EMD 74601-1 to 15

CC&O (CLINCHFIELD)

Road Number	Builder Date	Builder Number
3607 - 3618	11/72	7382-1 to 10
3617 - 3624	2/74	73773-1 to 8

SEABOARD SYSTEM

Road Number	Builder Date	Builder Number
8950-8964	Ex-SCL 2045-2059	
8965-8982	Ex-CRR 3607-3624	

SD45-2

In 1972, EMD released its latest locomotive to the railroads, the SD45-2. It was an upgraded version of the SD45, having the same prime mover and fuel capacity. Looking similar but different, the SD45-2 did not have flared ends on the long hood, just a flat continuation til the end. The three fans on the end of the long hood were spread out more along the roof.

The SCL units could be found system wide on the mainlines, moving freight mixed in with other locomotives in the consist. On the Clinchfield they were at home moving long, heavy coal trains south to Spartanburg, SC where their 3,600 horsepower came in handy while keeping to track speed.

SEABOARD COAST LINE SD45-2 #2059

FAMILY LINES SYSTEM SD45-2 #8976

SEABOARD SYSTEM SD45-2 #8966

CSX SD45-2 #8951

CSX SD45-2 #8954

CSX SD45-2 #8954

The reason for the book...

The memories of childhood are sometimes forgotten, put away like our toys, into boxes on shelves, but in our minds instead. So too, are the memories I have of these locomotives shown in this book. Grandma's house had the Seaboard Coast Line's line from Hamlet to Wilmington, NC. running right out in front of it. This is the place I fell in love with railroading, an affair that has accompanied me for most of my 51 years. Below is what I remember most...

Some trains went through in the day, and some at night. It was the ones at night that I look forward to the most.

It was here the trains were lit for viewing in the wee hours of the morning. Sleeping in the living room on the pull out couch, all I had to do was lift my head and before me laid a perfect view of all the action. If I were asleep, Daddy would wake me up as it seemed he always heard the trains before myself. There we would both sit up and take it all in. The Thundering loud air horns in the Carolina night beneath the long leaf pines and moonlit skies. Then came the ground-shaking earthquake as the locomotives rushed by. I will never forget the sight of the oscillating headlight on the lead locomotives as they passed, as if a Banshee searching through the night for its next victim. Right on the heels of all this would be the aroma of Diesel fumes drifting through the air. And before long, the mile long train bid me fair well as the caboose cleared the crossing. Then, as I laid back down to sleep, I heard the sound of the train as it made its way toward its distant terminal. a harmony of steel on steel which made a sound unique to my ears. Then slowly it died off into nothingness and disappeared. The again was the night left to be night, once more .

Daddy and Grandma have long since past, but the memories of them and the trains remain.

These locomotives were but a small variety of the ones who moved the freight, and the china in the Hutch every time they passed my Grandma's house. The color schemes depicted here are as close as I can get them, and therefore not exactly perfect, and for that I do in advance apologize. Memories aren't perfect either, but they can take you back to the places you want to go. As do my drawings take me back to the late 1970's and beyond. I have tried to include the original schemes of the locomotives, some of which were gone before my time.

It is my sincere hope you find enjoyment in looking into the pages of this book.

Daniel T. Edwards
Fuquay-Varina
3/29/2024

Made in United States
Orlando, FL
09 December 2024

55310219R00018